A Kalmyk Sampler: Mongol Poetry and Mythic Tale

Poems in English, Russian, and Kalmyk

Nikolai Burlakoff

Poetry by Rimma Khaninova

Illustrated by Eduardo Barrios

Translations by Carleton Copeland,
Erdni Eldyshev, Vera Shugraeva

A KALMYK SAMPLER:
MONGOL POETRY
AND MYTHIC TALE

Illustrations © Eduardo Barrios

All photos © Nick Olefer, Jr.

Ossining, NY

ISBN: 1479111635
ISBN-13: 978-1479111633

DEDICATION

This book is dedicated to women, in particular to Kalmyk and Russian women, who in the most trying circumstances and sometimes under horrific conditions gave all to protect their families and kept the fires of faith and culture burning.

CONTENTS

"One Million Prayers" Prayer Drum
Rashi Gempel-Ling Temple, Howell, New Jersey

ACKNOWLEDGMENTS

This is an international collaborative effort that involves writers and artists from Kalmykia, Russia, and the United States. Without the trust and goodwill of Rimma Khaninova, the poet who so readily responded to my request to use her poetry, we would not have the fruit of her work, nor would we have had the help of two other wonderful Kalmyk poets: Erdni Erdyshev and Vera Shugraeva. Rimma also brought on board the incomparable translator of her poetry, Carleton Copeland.

Eduardo Barrios is an artist who has forged a style of seeming simplicity that transmutes intense life challenges into lines that speak of peace, love, and serenity. It is a wonder to behold the way he carries that message in the artwork for a piece of writing that on first glance is as far from love and serenity as one can get. It is his art, however, that reminds us so clearly of the underlying central message of the words. We met a few years back on a project to share the wisdom of Nagarjuna, and most recently he unhesitatingly responded to my request to delve, with his vision and art, into the unfamiliar world of the nomad Kalmyks.

Gail S. Burlakoff has, in our thirty-year sojourn, been a rock of caring and support, who continually insists that I share what I know with anyone who is willing to listen. It is that faith in the message, and her practical skill of making the intentions and words clearer and more resonant, that is fundamental to the creation of this work.

The **Tulip Foundation** and its founding president, Naran Badushov, provided the needed sponsorship to ensure that beautiful dreams become a palpable reality, and that the rich culture of the Kalmyks becomes more widely known.

Mirror ball in St. Zonkava Temple
Philadelphia, Pennsylvania

INTRODUCTION

Miracles happen every day. Unfortunately, we ignore most of them. Who among us stops and allows him- or herself to be overwhelmed by the miracle of a flower growing out of a pile of dirt?

This book is a miracle. In the fall of 2009, when a friend and I visited a Kalmyk Buddhist temple in Howell, New Jersey, to observe the celebration of Zul (a Buddhist holiday totally unknown to me) I had no idea of the realities that would emerge from the visit.

To shorten a long story: the visit led to more than a year of fieldwork and deep immersion into research about the Kalmyks, and to quite a bit of writing about the group, their history, and their culture. All this work was a prelude to presenting Kalmyk culture at the New Jersey Folk Festival in April of 2011, something the NJFF board did to help the community celebrate their 60th anniversary in the United States.

The Festival was held and by all measures it was a resounding success: the first New Jersey Folk Festival at which a traditional epic song was performed, a traditional Buddhist ger (yurt) temple and a replica Kalmyk village (*khoton*) were erected, and not only did the Kalmyk Buddhist patriarch from Kalmykia (Russian Federation) attend, but virtually the entire Kalmyk community from New Jersey, New York, and Philadelphia was there.

One of the side benefits of this event is that many of the younger Kalmyks became more aware of some of the cultural treasures in their possession. One such treasure hangs in the vestibule of the Tashi Lhunpo Temple in Howell, NJ, to the left as one enters the door. This treasure, a yellow silk regimental flag of the so-called Dzhungarian Cavalry Regiment, was created during the Russian Civil War and accompanied the Kalmyk Cossacks as they evacuated from the Crimean peninsula in 1920. When I first saw it, it was covered with a plastic laundry bag to protect it from the elements. By the spring of 2012, however, the flag was encased in a solid wood and glass frame.

Little did I know, when I first saw it, how that flag would resonate in my life. I was intrigued by the blue central figure riding a mule. The figure had a necklace of skulls and a head hanging from the saddle. I asked my Kalmyk friends about the flag and they had no answers, so I asked the temple's monk. "Oh," he said, "That's Palden Lhamo, very powerful!" He beckoned me to follow him into the interior of the temple and showed me a small *thangka* (Tibetan icon) with a black creature depicted on a black background. "Very powerful," the monk said. "Protects this temple!"

Returning home I hit the Internet and began research. Soon I learned of Palden Lhamo (Tibetan), Sri Devi (Indian), and Okon Tengri (Kalmyk), as well as Erlik Khan, the Mongolian god of the underworld.

The first three names are those of the same female protector deity, the consort of the god of the underworld. There was something strangely fascinating in learning the story of this fierce *drag-gshed* (protector goddess) who killed and flayed her son, and drank his blood to protect humankind from destruction. Fascinating, also, to learn that despite her fierceness and violation of human maternal expectations, she is much venerated and seen as the mother of everything. In Mongolia, children leave bits of ice for her steed when she rides by on the eve of Tsagan Sar, marking the liberation of the spring sun from the underworld.

I found a magic tale (folktales that most English speakers call "fairy tales") called "The Story of the Tsagan Sar Holiday." Tsagan Sar, which literally means "White Month," refers to the Mongolian New Year celebration that lasts a whole month. In the tale we encounter Okon Tengri, who kills the monster son of Nogan Dara-eke-gegyan (Green Tara).

This is a classic magic tale, in which a dire situation (a monster eating the people) is remedied by the hero/heroine, who undergoes difficult trials, but with the assistance of a magical helper (Okon Tengri), perseveres and triumphs. Thanks to the victory of the heroine, social norms are restored.

The story is a rare beauty—a combination of reality (actual celebrations), the mythic Okon Tengri, and the enlightened beauty, Nogan Dara-eke-gegyan. I translated the tale in hopes of creating a chapbook of the Kalmyk tales for the NJ Folk Festival; that was not accomplished.

In spring of 2012 I contacted Rimma Khaninova, a well-known Kalmyk poet, and asked for permission to post her poem about Okon Tengri next to the flag in Howell, to explain the significance of the image. Later, I went to Rimma's website to look for lines of poetry for my planned book and immediately came upon her poem about Zul, the Kalmyk New Year.

Sometimes ideas take years to take shape; sometimes they spring fully formed, like Athena from the head of Zeus. And so it happened here. Seeing the "Zul" poem I suddenly envisioned the tale of Tsagan Sar bookended by Rimma Khaninova's "Okon Tengri" and "Zul" poems—a continuity from ancestral Zul, through mythic tale, to modern poem of powerful and redeeming feminine principle; a triad, in fact, reminiscent of the traditional iron tripod used by Kalmyks to hold the life-giving cook's kettle and to demarcate the living fire within the ger (yurt).

Another letter to Rimma, and another wonderful and generous response; not only allowing me to use the poems but adding another poem, one on Tsagan Sar. More correspondence followed, and Rimma was able to involve not only her excellent translator, Carlton Copeland, but also two other Kalmyk poets, Vera Shugraeva and Erdni Eldyshev who made their contribution by translating Rimma's poems from Russian to Kalmyk.

Suddenly, we had three first-class poems in Kalmyk, Russian, and English as well as a complex and unusual folktale that touched the mythic world of ancient shamanistic realities, more recent Buddhist conceptions, and the spiritual aspiration of the Kalmyk people.

Our project needed someone who could give a visual sense of the world of the Kalmyk nomads and the spirit world of Mongolian Buddhism. Fortunately, I have a friend, an immigrant from Uruguay, an artist and a fellow Buddhist whom I could ask for help. To my delight Eduardo Barrios was willing to take-on the challenge and joined our team—creating, in essence, a wonderful syncretism of differing times, worldviews, cultures, and languages, but unified in an endeavor reflecting a "community of altruism," to use Pitirim Sorokin's terminology.

Eduardo's challenge was to learn, in a very short period of time, some of the ethnographic specifics of Kalmyk culture so as to create images that would resonate within the culture and give solid information to novices. In that, he largely succeeded. I take responsibility for any errors that may have crept into the image of Green Tara. The fault is mine, not his. The Internet is a wonderful tool, without which this book would have never become reality, but long-distance communication within very constricted time limits will lead to errors.

And so this is the story of how our little book came into being; an extraordinary everyday miracle, like the prairie bluebells by the road—just as improbable and inevitable. As Geshe Tenzin, the monk at Tashi Lhunpo Temple said, "Okon Tengri is very powerful"; and as my wife, in her inimitable style, said, "When you have a black figure on a black background—very powerful."

The Kalmyks, ancestrally the Oirat people, originated in the Altai Mountains (East Central Asia). 1608 is considered to be the official date of their entering the Russian sphere of influence north of the Caspian Sea and between the Volga and Don rivers. The golden age of Kalmyks is traditionally thought to be the reign of Ayuka Khan (1669–1724). In 1771, under Ubashi Khan, the majority of Kalmyks migrated from Russia to the Manchu Empire in China. About half of the returnees perished on the journey, those who survived became the forebears of today's Kalmyks in China's Xinjiang province.

After 1771 the Kalmyk Khanate was dissolved, and the increasing population on traditional Kalmyk pastureland led to a decline in the economic well-being of the group. Some Kalmyks entered the Russian Cossack estate (formal class designation) and formed a new Kalmyk sub-group: the Buzava. During the Russian Civil War Kalmyks, predominantly of the Buzava clan, sided with the counter-revolutionary forces and were forced in 1920 to leave Crimea with the

Whites. They settled in Bulgaria (Sofia), Czechoslovakia (Prague), France (Paris and Lyon); most of them settled in Belgrade, Serbia, where they built a Buddhist temple in 1929.

World War II led to two major upheavals among the Kalmyks. Those who resettled in Eastern Europe and the Balkans were forced to relocate, once more, to avoid the approaching Soviet Army. On December 27, 1943, the Kalmyks in Kalmykia were gathered by the internal security forces and dispersed across the Soviet Union, predominantly throughout Siberia and Kazakhstan. On that day the Kalmyk Autonomous Republic ceased to exist, and Kalmyk lands were apportioned by the Soviet government among neighboring governmental entities. Therefore, between 1944 and 1957, a sense of group identity and communal cultural life existed only in the diaspora communities.

Refugees, most of whom were in the Schleissheim and Ingolstadt DP camps in West Germany, languished for six years (1945-1951) because they did not want to resettle as individuals, or as separate families, and no country wanted to allow a group of Kalmyks to immigrate.

In August, 1951, the Acting Attorney General of the United States upheld the Board of Immigration Appeals decision that had overturned a previous adverse ruling of a special inquiry board holding a Kalmyk couple ineligible to immigrate. Initially they were denied immigrant status because they were not members of the "white" race. The 1951 decision declared them to be European and therefore "white," making the Kalmyks the only "white" Mongols in the world. As a consequence, nearly 600 Kalmyks came to the U.S. between 1951 and 1952.

The historical irony is that between 1951 and 1957, when the Kalmyk Autonomous Republic was reestablished in the Soviet Union, Kalmyks in America where the only organized Kalmyk community outside of Xinjiang, China.

In 1952 the Kalmyks in Howell, New Jersey, organized the first Tibeto-Mongolian Buddhist congregation and established the first such temple in the U.S. During the next 20 years three other temples were built in Howell, and another in Philadelphia, Pennsylvania; a monastery was established in Howell, moved first to New Brunswick and then to Washington Township, New Jersey, where it flourishes today as the Tibetan Buddhist Learning Center.

Some 60 years--roughly three generations--later, the Kalmyks have survived and prospered in America. Some additional immigration occurred in the 1960's, and a larger influx of immigrants came after the collapse of the Soviet Union in 1991. Today an estimated 1,000 to 3,000 Kalmyks live in the United States, with approximately 300 around the Howell, New Jersey, area.

The American generation of Kalmyks (those in their 40's today) is keen to learn more about their history and culture, preserving the artifacts and cultural expressions of their community, and working to overcome the traditional fractiousness of the older generation. Some concrete steps have been taken to realize these aspirations. In 2010, the Kalmyks from Howell, New York, and Philadelphia came together to showcase their community at the New Jersey Folk Festival, which took place in 2011. In the 60 years that Kalmyks have been in America, this was the first community-wide sharing of Kalmyk culture before 15,000 non-Kalmyk festival attendees.

In 2012 the Kalmyk communities in the U.S. and Kalmykia were invited to participate in the 2013 Smithsonian Folklife Festival in Washington, D.C., to raise the American public's awareness of the fragility of the languages and cultures of many indigenous peoples around the world. UNESCO considers the Kalmyk language to be endangered. This slender volume is our contribution to the effort of raising awareness of the problem and also providing an insight into the poetic, mythic, and traditional worlds of the Kalmyks.

Nitsan Temple, Howell, New Jersey

Zul, 2009 – Tashi Lhunpo Temple, Howell, New Jersey

Rimma Khaninova

ZUL

Ancestral mystery, festive Zul
has fanned the holy flame anew –
a prayer of heart and mind as one:
the Kalmyk winter has begun!
Henceforth the way be white ahead.
Unbroken be life's vital thread.
Let light prevail as shades descend.
May kin and riches know no end.
May wisdom be forever young.
May age, rewarding, gently come.
Around the family hearth be peace,
and bread with milk not bittersweet.
May foemen, changing heart, concede,
and friends be true in times of need.
May humankind be justly known
as wise for ages yet to come!
Ancestral mystery, festive Zul,
you've never failed to see us through
as down the ages burns the same
beguiling, purifying flame!

December 26, 1992
Translated by Carleton Copeland.

Zul, 2010 – Tashi Lhunpo Temple, Howell, New Jersey

Римма Ханинова

ЗУЛ

О тайна предков, праздник Зул,
огонь священный вновь раздул,
молитва сердца и ума:
зима калмыцкая пришла!
Да будет белым новый путь,
да не прервется жизни суть,
да будет свет в преддверье тьмы,
добро и свет не сочтены.
Да будет мудрость молода,
а старость в радости легка,
да будет мирным отчий дом,
а хлеб не горьким с молоком.
Да будут кротки все враги,
друзья в беде всегда верны,
да будет зваться человек
разумным много тысяч лет!
Ты тайна предков, праздник Зул,
ты никого не обманул.
Горит огонь твой сквозь века,
вновь очищая и маня!

26 декабря 1992
Теегин герл. – 2008. – № 8. – С. 2.

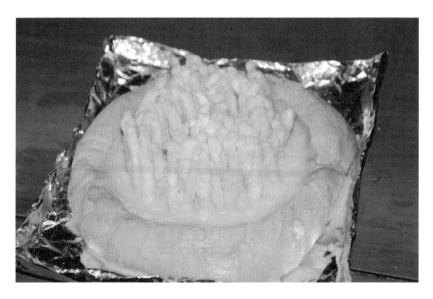

"Ancestor Boat" – Zul, 2010

Ханина Римма

ЗУЛ

Өвкнрин нуувцин ицг болсн
Олнд темдгтə Зулын өдрт
Əмтнə зүркнə, ухана зальврһн
Əрүн һал дəкнəс шатава.
Хальмгт үвл ирвə.
Шин хаалһ цаһан болтха,
Җирһлин чинр бичə тасртха,
Харңһун өмнəс герл ортха,
Хамгин сəнь делгрəд йовтха,
Керсү ухатань шинрəд бəəтхə,
Көгшрх насн байрар дүүртхə,
Төрскн һазр төвкнүн җирһтхə,
Тоһш, үсн элвəд бəəтхə.
Дəəлдх дəəсн номһн болтха,
Нəəҗнр зовлңгд итклтə болтха,
Миңһəд җилмүд һатлад күн
Мергн, цецнəрн туурч йовтха.
Герл өгсн Зулын һал
Һазр деерк əмтə тоотыг
Насни туршарт цеврлəд əдслнə,
Насни туршарт нəəлвр өгнə!

Орчулснь Шугран Вера.

11

Rimma Khaninova

OKON TENGRI[1]

Celestial maiden of fire,
so gentle and fair of face,
your tale is a mystery entire
to me, privy now to your ways.
Quintessence of feminine kind
(capricious life's path, is it not?),
but you, as the Mangus king's bride,
did violence to your own heart.
And so, when a child, nature's gift,
was due to come into this world,
you, plagued not a little by guilt,
were true to your instinct, your word,
and slew your own son, who in time
was meant to devour man's race.
So shattered was she by her crime,
a grimace contorted her face,
her skin, turning blue, lost its gleam,
and so, in an instant transformed –
her eyes bulging out, wild as screams –
a fearsome *dokshita* was born.
This deity savage and wroth,
defense against foes, sits astride
a mule on a grim saddle cloth
composed of her baby's flayed hide,
and, pressing the flesh of her flesh,
she hurries to bring to the Earth
a spring that has long been withheld
by crafty Erlik Nomin Khan[2].

---

[1] Okon Tengri is a sky goddess (*tengri*). Taken as wife by the king of the demonic Mangus, she slew her own son, who was to destroy humankind, and so became a wrathful deity (*dokshita*), defender of the faith. One legend has it that spring comes each year when she restores the sun swallowed by Erlik Nomin Khan.

[2] Erlik Nomin Khan, Lord of the Dead in Mongolian and Turkic pantheons, is a wrathful deity identified with the Hindu and Buddhist god Yama.

Are you, lady savior of all,
a butcher or victim?
Who knows?
Your sins as a mother appall,
but I have no heart to cast stones.
Dilemmas of virtue and sin –
the touchstone of feeling and mind –
resemble dead coals that yet hide
an ember of frenzy within.

February 20, 1994
Translated by Carleton Copeland

Palden Lhamo *thangka*

Римма Ханинова

ОКОН-ТЕНГРИ

Небесная дева огня,
прекрасная ликом своим,
ты – тайна теперь для меня,
причастной к загадкам твоим.
Ты – женственность, нежность сама,
(о, сколь прихотлив жизни путь!)
женой всех мангусов царя
неволила бренную суть.
Когда дар природы, дитя,
увидеть был должен сей свет,
нимало себя не виня,
сдержала инстинкт свой, завет,
и сына убила, ведь он –
был призван губить людской род.
Злодейством ум так потрясен,
что им искривлен ее рот,
а кожа, став синею вмиг,
утратила свежесть и цвет,
глаз выкатив дикий, как вскрик,
докшита явилалась в ответ.
Свирепое то божество –
защита людей от врагов,
ногою свое естество –
всю кожу ребенка – покров
мула белого сжав,
торопит на землю весну,
которую задержал
коварный Эрлик-номин-хан

О женщина, спасшая всех,
палач ты иль жертва?
Как знать…
Но твой материнский грех
мне с горечью сложно признать.
Дилемма добра и зла –
критерий ума и чувств, –
как мертвая вроде зола
скрывает свой уголь буйств.

20 февраля 1994
День влюбленных: сб. стихов.
– Элиста, 1997.С. 159-160.

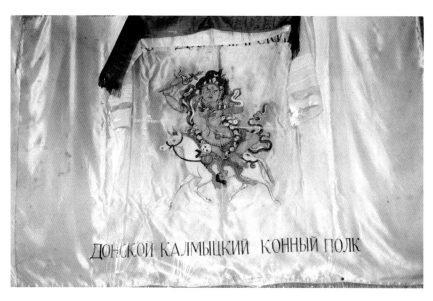

Flag of the 80th Don Kalmyk Cavalry regiment - Dzhungarian

Okon Tengri riding sidesaddle on her mule

Ханина Римма

ОКН-ТЕҢГР

Һээхмҗ болгсн сээхн чирэтэ
Һалын теңгрин окн,
Тана нуувчиг аңхрдг болвчн,
Та бийдм бүтү заңгтат.
Әрүн күүкд улсин хүвлһэн
(Әмдрлин хаалһ адрута болна!)
Әср маңһсдын хаана хатн
Әмтэ хамгт күч үзүлнэт.
Теңгрин хээрн – алтн үрнь
Төрх саам учрсн кемлэ,
Эвдх килнцэс сүрдл уга,
Экин буйнч седклэн дарҗ,
Күмни эмнд күрх заята
Көвүһэн эн эврэн хораҗ.
Әвд йовдлас ухань сүрдэд,
Амнь тер уханас коочиҗ,
Арснь болхла, агчмд көкрэд,
Әмтин сээхн өңгэн гееҗ.
Алң болгсн нүдэн бүлтэҗ
Аштнь догшн аһ үүдҗ.
Догшн сэкүстэ эн бурхн –
Дээснэс эмтнд харслт болв.
Эн – нилхин арста цаһан
Элҗгниг көлэрн шахҗ,
Эрлг номин хан тушсн
Ээлтэ хавриг угтҗ дуудна.
О, күмниг аврсн күүкд күн,
Та – алачвт, аль меңгвт?
Тааҗ яһҗ медхв…
Зуг нанд һарһсн килнцинтн
Зөвинь медхд амр биш.
Хээр болн хар санан –
Ухана болн седклин кемҗэн –
Цеңкиҗ киитрсн үмсн доран
Цог хадһлсн мет болна.

Орчулснь Эльдшэ Эрднь.

Palden Lhamo *thangka*

Rimma Khaninova

TSAGAN SAR, THE WHITE MONTH

In holy awe Kalmyks would greet the light
that blessed their land and made it thrive and bloom.
They prayed in reverence, grateful at the sight:
Okon Tengri had saved the world from gloom.
The offerings prepared for the occasion
showed veneration for the gods who'd seen
the camp and livestock through the winter season,
that they might be as merciful again.
"You wintered well?" Kalmyks were asked in greeting.
"Quite well, quite well," they each in turn replied.
The words reveal an underlying meaning:
all blessings to all beings far and wide.
When meeting, they would ritually clasp
the arms of those they met; thus young and old
convinced themselves that spring had come at last
and they'd been spared by hunger, plague and cold.
They made spring visits, honoring tradition,
to each in order of seniority,
And rings of *bortsik*s were their way of wishing[3]
to each good fortune and prosperity.
May dust not ever gather at your door,
and each guest be a blessing in your sight.
May nomads see the prairie dog once more
and find the way ahead forever white.
May bonfires burn anew with fire that cleanses.
May cow chips under trivets not go cold.
Spring tells us, by appealing to the senses,
that we're alive to feel the joy unfold!
O may your day be radiant and sure
to turn aside fate's blows and banish strife!
O may the White Month be forever pure –
our forebears' gift, the holiday of life!

August 17, 2012
Translated by Carleton Copeland

---

[3] Bortsiks are pieces of dough fried in boiling fat, similar to doughnuts. Strung together in loops, they were given as holiday gifts.

Tashi Lhunpo Temple, Howell, New Jersey – Tsagan Sar, 2010

Римма Ханинова

ЦАГАН САР – БЕЛЫЙ МЕСЯЦ

Встречая с трепетом божественным светило, –
источник благоденствия земли –
калмыки благодарные молили;
спасла все сущее навек Окон-Тенгри.
Богам жертвоприношение готово –
почет и уваженье – деежи,
пусть милостивы будут к людям снова:
кочевье, скот зимою сберегли.
Традиционное приветствие калмыков:
– Менде гарва? – Менде, менде.
В нем заключен глубокий смысл:
благополучие во всем и вся – везде.
Рукопожатья ритуал свершая,
касаются при встрече стар и млад,
чтоб убедиться – все весну встречают:
их миновали голод, мор и хлад.
Хожденье по гостям с весенним поздравленьем –
в особой очередности почет,
и связка борцыков с древнейшим назначеньем
пусть изобилие и счастье принесет.
Пусть пыль не оседает у порога –
благословенен в доме каждый гость.
Пусть станет белою кочевнику дорога,
увидеть суслика ему чтоб довелось.
Пусть вновь горят костры всеочищенья,
кизяк не гаснет век под таганом.
Весна пришла с соблазном ощущенья –
блаженство счастья – мы с тобой живем!
Пусть будет день для вас лучистым,
пусть отвратит от вас судьбы удар!
Пусть Белый Месяц будет вечно чистым–
священной жизни праздник, предков дар!

4 февраля 1994
День влюбленых: сб. стихов.
– Элиста, 1997. – С. 169-170

Breaking fast with Kalmyk tea, Tsagan Sar morning – Tashi Lhunpo temple

Ханина Римма

ЦАҺАН САР

Орчлңгин кеермҗ – нарна урһциг
Оларн хальмгуд күндлҗ тосна.
Әмтиг аврсн Окн-Теңгрт
Әрүн ханлтан өргҗ зальврна.
Олн бурхдт деежән өргнә,
Өршәңгү тедн әмтиг евәтхә:
Үвләр хошинь, малынь хадһлтха.
«Үвләс менд һарвта?» – гиж
Уул авъясар хальмгуд менддлнә.
«Менд, сән һарвидн» – болҗ
Маасхлзҗ инәлдәд хәрү өгнә.
Эн авъяс гүн учрта:
Эв, амулң цугтаднь дурдна.
Ик-баһнь ханцан атхсн,
Ирх җирһл угтҗ цаһална.
Хавриг цуһар байрлҗ тосна:
Хавҗңндг, өлсдг цаг давв.
Цаһалхар хальмгуд гиичд одцхана,
Цаһана боорцган эдн белглнә.
Хуучн эн өвкнрин заңшалзц
Хөв-кишг заях болтха.
Эркин өмн тоосн бүргтхә –
Эгл гиич болһн күндтә.
Теегин күүнә хаалһнь цаһатха,
Терүнд хаврин зурмн харһтха.
Цевр зальта дендр астха,
Туlһ дор арһсн шаттха.
Күслд җивр урһадг хавр
Күмнд хөвтә җирһл учратха!
Өдр болһнтн ээлтә болтха,
Өшрлһн, зовлһн холаһар һартха!
Цаглшго зөөр, әдстә байр –
Цаһан Сар өлзә дурдтха!

Орчуlснь Эльдшә Эрднь.

23

Nogan Dara-eke-gegyan (Green Tara)

THE STORY OF THE TSAGAN SAR HOLIDAY

This was long ago. In those days a black hump-backed *mangas* (ogre) attacked people. Nogan Dara-eke-gegyan , who was so unbelievably beautiful that one could graze cattle and sew in the radiance emanating from her, decided to save the people from destruction.

Nogan Dara-eke found out when the *mangas* would arrive and she met him. The *mangas* and Nogan Dara-eke became husband and wife. A year later a son was born to them. But Nogan Dara-eke did not forget that she had to destroy the *mangas*.

And so, one day when her son was lying next to her, she pricked him with an awl. Hearing his son's crying the *mangas* asked Nogan Dara-eke, "Why is my son crying?" Nogan Dara-eke replied, "Your son wants to unite his soul with yours." The

25

mangas responded that his own soul was located in the three legs of a small calf, but Nogan Dara-eke did not believe him.

Once more she made their son cry by pricking him with an awl. The boy started crying loudly and the *mangas* asked why he was crying. Nogan Dara-eke explained to the *mangas*, "Your son does not believe that your soul is located so far away, and that is why he is crying so bitterly." But the crafty *mangas* responded this time that his soul was in the corner of the pillow. The boy began to cry even more than before and,

again, Nogan Dara-eke informed the *mangas* about the cause of their son's crying, "He does not believe that your soul is in the pillow."

The *mangas* decided to tell his son and wife the truth about his soul, and said, "My soul is found in a wooden chest, on the side where the sun sets, in a deep pit that is dug at the foot of the mountain; in a wooden chest there is a small iron chest, and in the small iron chest, a silver one, in which three fledglings are living. These three fledglings are my soul." Saying these words, the *mangas* uttered a *kharal* (curse), "He who sees it—let him be immediately blinded and he who hears these words—let him become deaf."

Soon the *mangas* fell into a deep sleep. Nogan Dara-eke went to the foot of the mountain to find the soul of the *mangas*. She dug a deep pit, found the small chests containing his souls, and opened them. Out flew the three fledglings. Then Nogan

Dara-eke loosened upon the earth an iron rain and on her right hand she lit the sun. And the three fledglings sat on her palm. She caught the fledglings and immediately strangled one of them.

She set out to return home, and on the way there she killed another fledgling. With a single fledgling in her hand she paused at the threshold of her home and heard the groaning of the *mangas* reaching heaven and earth. And next to the groaning *mangas* she strangled the last fledgling. The *mangas* died immediately. Nogan Dara-eke burned the corpse of the *mangas*, but first she cut off his head.

Suddenly a harrier bird came through the smoke hole of the yurt. This made Nogan Dara-eke happy and she wrote a letter and tied it to the wing of the harrier. In the letter she wrote that she eliminated the evil *mangas*, who destroyed many people. She said that she needed a saddled white horse so that she could return home. The harrier bird flew to Nogan Dara-eke's native land and delivered the letter. The people were happy and they sent an equipped horse.

Time passed, and Nogan Dara-eke went home, tying the head of the *mangas* to the saddle and taking her son with her. She travelled for a long time; reaching the land of Bayin-dala (in today's Sinkiang province), she left her son there and she continued without him.

At that time people asked the heavenly maiden, Okon Tengri, to greet Nogan Dara-eke. When Okon Tengri met her she asked Nogan Dara-eke, "Did you leave someone in a far-distant land?" Nogan Dara-eke understood that she was being asked about her son, and she hesitated with her answer. Okon Tengri told her, "Don't hide it. You have a son. But

this is a son of *mangas!* You must kill him!" They returned to the place where the son of Nogan Dara-eke was.

Seeing Okon Tengri, the son of the *mangas* attacked her. Okon Tengri began to chop him into pieces which, in the battle, turned into one large stone. At the end of a long struggle, the son of the *mangas* began to defeat Okon Tengri.

And then Nogan Dara-eke confided in Okon Tengri, "Between his shoulder blades is a small hole, which is where his soul lies. Tear it out by the root!" Okon Tengri put her finger into the hole and tore out the soul of the little *mangas*. Before his end the boy said, "I regret that I did not reach the age of ten months. Then I could have taken revenge on everyone for Father."

Having defeated all enemies, Nogan Dara-eke and Okon Tengri arrived in the early morning on the sunny breeze to their native *nutuk*-land and began to greet everyone by shaking hands with them. And in honor of their victory, although the day, month, and year when Nogan Dara-eke and Okon Tengri arrived were considered inauspicious, the people decided to give them an auspicious name. From that time on they called the month white, and good: "Tsagan Sar."

On that day people began to awaken at dawn, when the lines on the palm of the hand are barely visible. And from then on they began to greet each other by offering their hand to, and asking: "Did you come out of the cold winter well?"

From that time on people began to call the courageous heavenly maiden, Okon Tengri, a guardian and warrior: Daichi.

On the day of Tsagan Sar people utter the poetic blessing (iorel):

> May there be on this bright day
> much, much white food,
> and we will happily greet Tsagan Sar.
> May the drink of immortality (*arshan*)—the magic nectar,
> be there for all people.
> Live happily and in meritorious actions
> all the years that you are given!

HOLIDAYS

Zul

When we visited Tashi Lhunpo temple in Howell, New Jersey, in the autumn of 2009, neither my friend, Shelley Blitstein, a practicing Buddhist in the Tibetan tradition, nor I, an adherent of Vietnamese Zen, had any idea of what the Zul festival represents in Kalmyk culture. I may have discovered, through some research on the Internet before our visit, that this was a celebration of Je Tsongkhapa's birthday, but that said little to me, although I knew that Tsongkhapa had founded the *Gelug-pa* Buddhist tradition in Tibet. Only much later, and with the help of Elza Petrovna Bakaeva's seminal study, *Buddhism in Kalmykia*[4], did I learn that Zul was the ancient shamanistic New Year and that the Buddhist overlay represents classic religious syncretism.

An 1852 description gives a nice feel for the holiday in days when the Kalmyks still followed their nomadic ways:

> *"The second annual holiday is "Zul," which is always celebrated on the 24th day of the month "Bar-sar" (month of the snow leopard) which comes near the end of our November. This festival is celebrated by the Kalmyks to inaugurate the winter and the day of their New Year.*
>
> *Zul is especially remarkable for us because it is on this day that all Kalmyks commemorate their birthdays. If a Kalmyk had a son born a week before Zul, then on the day of Zul he is considered to be in his second year from birth; at next Zul his second year will be counted as the third, etc.*
>
> *On Zul, religious activities begin in the evening, in the open steppe; on which, near the khurul (temple), a large table is placed. Each Kalmyk arrives here from his ger (moveable felt and wood domicile), bringing with him a cup made out of dough [and] filled with melted cow's butter and a wick, and places it on the table.*
>
> *In the meanwhile, in the khurul a worship service is in progress; when the*

---

[4] Elza Petrovna Bakaeva. Buddizm v kalmykii: isoriko-etnograficheskie ocherki (*Buddhism in Kalmykia: Historico-ethnographic Sketches*) Elista: Kalmykia, Kalmytskoe knizhnoe izdatel'stvo, 1997.

gelugs (Kalmyk Buddhist priests) exit from it, and while carrying burkhans (holy images), begin to circumambulate the gers [yurts] singing all the while, accompanied by with loud music; the people bow before the burkhans, each one lights his cup, and begins to pray.

For this evening festive illumination is arranged; from top to the bottom, from the inside and out, all khuruls are blazing with light: poor Kalmyks pass long poles through the tsagryk (ger vent opening) and hang on these specially made dough cups in which melted cow butter is burning. Among the rich all gers are as if bathed in streams of light.

At the end of the worship service the people go to visit their acquaintances and everyone congratulates each other with the New Year.

The Kalmyks hold an election on this day among the gelungs for a new gebke (abbot), an office respected by the people. After the election there follow special religious ceremonies and the festivities conclude with general merriment in which neither horse racing, nor wrestling, are allowed by tradition."[5]

At Tashi Lhunpo the monks began to light tea candles instead of butter lamps, and asked those who came for the service to assist. Shelley and I did, but when everyone else left the temple to go outside I followed and saw people clustered around a metal-covered table on which objects had been placed. One man, who I later learned was Dave, began to light the objects with a hand-held gas torch. Everyone stood quietly, looking on. I was taking photographs; smelling burnt flour, I asked, "Is that bread, burning?" "It's dough," replied one of the ladies in the group.

The flames went out and everyone went back inside the temple, which now was bathed in light from the many tea lights. The service went on for more than an hour, with more people arriving until the interior of the small temple was pretty much filled. Two monks kept chanting prayers in Tibetan. During the service the older folk prayed, and many whispered among themselves. A few of the younger children played hand-held video games. A handful of *malas* (Buddhist prayer beads) hung from a nail driven into one of the four painted posts surrounding the central atrium. People took those beads, used them to pray, and then hung them up again. I observed a number of people, especially among the more elderly, who upon entry into the temple girded themselves with a sash or belt.

Toward the end of the service the senior monk called on one of the men to come forward and hold a tray with offerings. Shortly afterward, the senior monk ended the service by delivering a short homily about Tsongkhapa's birthday and his importance to Buddhism. Afterwards, a number of people in the congregation were recognized for their work for the temple and were awarded white silk *khatas* (Tib.; *khadyk*-Kalm.), long scarves given as a blessing and thank you.

After that, the congregation began to troop toward the altar, first making prostrations before it, then walking up to the monks, who were sitting at a long table

[5] Paul Nebol'sin, compiler Ocherki byta kalmykov khoshutovkago ulusa (*Sketches of the Life of the Kalmyks in the Khoshutov Ulus*), St. Petersburg, 1852 pp. 121-122

at the left of the atrium and perpendicular to the altar. Everyone placed before each monk a monetary offering, usually a dollar bill (although some gave a $20 bill.) One monk would bless the donor with a touch of a peacock feather and a second (more senior) monk would pour a liquid into the cupped hands of the congregant. That liquid was then brought up to the congregant's lips and then poured over his or her head.

Next, everyone went up to the altar, placed coins in front of chosen images, mumbled quick prayers and, one-by-one, left the temple; once outside, most people circumambulated the temple three times, clockwise. Afterwards, everyone went to the nearby parish hall.

Shelly and I stayed-back. I was intrigued by an East Asian-looking wooden statue of Kuan Yin, which stood at the right side of the altar. As the senior monk, *manya* Tenzin emerged (only American Kalmyks use the term *manya* to denote Buddhist monks) I asked him about the statue. "Oh," he said, "that was a donation sent to the temple from a member who was in the Vietnam War." The *manya*, and we, proceeded to the parish hall.

Inside the hall everyone was laughing, talking, and eating. A large stockpot, now almost half-full of Kalmyk tea, stood steaming. As I learned later, Kalmyk tea is the first dish traditionally offered on Zul.

Sometime, very long ago, there lived a wise man named Zonkava (Tsongkhapa), who for many years suffered from a severe disease.

Once Zonkava went to a famous healer; he examined Zonkava and said:

"A divine drink will enable you to cure this disease."

"What kind of drink?"

"A strong and fragrant tea with milk and salt. Drink it on an empty stomach for seven days."

Zonkava began to make and drink that tea, and his health got better and better until the day came when the disease left him. That happened on the 25th day of the first winter month according to the lunar calendar. Zonkava arose from his bed, and went out into the fresh air, and could not have been happier about the wide world and his miraculous healing from a deadly disease.

From then on, at Zonkava's command, each year on the 25th day of the first winter month, the Kalmyks commemorate the Zul holiday. On that day all Kalmyks from small to large add one year to their age. To honor the holy images, vigil lights are lit and the ritual offering of tea is made that day. The divine drink granted to the Kalmyks from that time on was called Kalmyk tea or dzhomba and was considered be the first treat. When the elders drink the tea on the Zul holiday they utter the following blessing and good-wishes:

Commemorating each year
Zul and Tsgan Sar,
Imbibing Zonkava's
Noble nectar,
I take a place
In the midst of

The six forms of life,
May we live one hundred years!
From that time on the following saying has been popular among the people—
"Tea, though liquid, is the head of all dishes; paper, though thin, is the servant of
knowledge and learning."[6]

I found Rita, a Kalmyk lady who had relatively recently arrived from Russia and whom I had met earlier that afternoon, and she offered us Kalmyk tea and *bortsek*. We learned that, in Howell, Kalmyk tea is made with butter and a bit of nutmeg, in addition to the milk. One lady gravely advised me that, for the best-tasting tea, whipped butter is best.

Rita introduced us to Tsagan and David, her relatives, who are very active in the temple. We began talking about the possibility of getting the Kalmyk community involved in the coming year's New Jersey Folk Festival. Our appearance was fortuitous, since the community was beginning to think about how to celebrate the 60th anniversary of the arrival of Kalmyks to the United States, in 1951.

Later, another friend, Alta, a parishioner at the St. Zonkava temple in Philadelphia, shared with me a prayer associated with Zul:

Mik Med Tsey We Ter Chen Chanrezig
Dri Med Kyen Be Wang Bo Jambeyang
Dit Poong Mallee Jum Dzad Sangwee Dak
Kangchan Khi Pi Tsig Gyan Tsong Khapa
Lozang Dakbi Zhab La Sol Ba Deb[7]

This is a Tibetan prayer. Since there was no training of Kalmyk monks during the years of Soviet rule, all Kalmyk temples in the U.S. installed Tibetan clergy after the immigrant generation of clergy died. This has led to a number of interesting dynamics within the community, dynamics that lie outside the scope of this book

Alta also shared some of the family rituals that are followed in his house before Zul. One involves taking a bath or shower, drying oneself with an old piece of clothing (such as an old T-shirt) and then piercing it with a needle and throwing it away. As Alta added, "the meaning of the needle has been lost, but the fact that we keep the ritual is most important."[8]

Shelley and I left after a while. As we drove back to New York he said, "You know, I missed the first night of Hanukkah tonight, but that's OK; I felt as if I were in *shul* tonight."

In 2010 the Zul celebration was even more interesting to me. By that time I was

---

[6] "Zul" legend in: D.E. Basaev. Sem zvezd: kalmytskie legendy i predaniya (*Seven Stars: Kalmyk Legends and Traditions*), Elista: Kalm., Kalm. kn. izd-vo, 2004, str. 75-76.

[7] Personal communication with Augnel "Alta" Burushkin, 2010.

[8] After reading an early draft of this article, Alta, at the 2012 Maitreya Festival informed me that he now knew the reason for discarding the needle—it was a carrier of evil.

more knowledgeable and knew what to pay attention to, and although some members of the community found my insatiable curiosity a bit irritating, many were invigorated by my interest and seemed to take more care and pride in following their traditions. Rita, who works as a nurse at a local hospital, could not leave her shift for the 2010 Zul celebration, but her husband, George, who confessed himself to be not much of a cook, proudly brought an "ancestor boat" he, himself, had made from dough and butter.

And this is my experience with Zul, the ancient New Year of the Kalmyks, it would have been impossible to predict all the events and multiple realities that the first trip would generate. For me it definitely opened a new "year" in life.

Tsagan Sar

The most important Kalmyk festival, Tsagan Sar (White Month), begins on the first day of the first lunar month. It celebrates spring and the end of winter.

Many traditional customs are associated with this holiday: on the eve of Tsagan, leaving three pieces of ice outside the ger (yurt) for Okon Tengri's mule; breaking fast with Kalmyk tea and ritual fry bread (*bortsek*) formed in the shape of the sun; eating white food; visiting relatives, from older to younger; a special ritual greeting of clasping both arms; and others. There is also a complete identification of Okon Tengri with this holiday. All this is true not only among the Kalmyks but also among all the different Mongol groups.

Among Mongols in Mongolia and China, and among Tibetans, the holiday is a celebration of the New Year. Among Kalmyks in America, everyone I met also considers this holiday as a New Year's celebration. Since Zul is the traditional Kalmyk New Year, the American tradition of also treating Tsagan as a New Year creates a cultural practice of two such holidays--something that brought a degree of confusion and discomfort among the informants I talked to.

I also was confused and thought that I stumbled on a rare culture group that had two traditional New Years. It dawned on me only recently that Tsagan Sar is not a New Year celebration. Perhaps my misunderstanding was reinforced by the fact that gift-giving is a tradition among American Kalmyks, as is a large community-wide dance. The latter is a tradition that was inaugurated by Kalmyks in the Displaced Persons camps in Germany after WWII, one they borrowed from their Russian neighbors in those camps.

In earlier times Tsagan entertainment was more vigorous, at least among the Buzava, or Don Kalmyks. One tradition maintained until the Russian revolution was a cavalry game in which young men of a village, mounted on horseback, would divide into two groups and clash, trying to unseat each other with the use of the traditional Kalmyk *malya* (whip). Older men, women, and girls would urge the young men on. Considering that Kalmyks began riding horses at the age of three, and that by five years of age they were full-fledged working members of the family, by the time they reached military age they were superb horsemen, fully versed in the use of the *malya*, which sometimes served as a sabre substitute. There are stories from the Russo-Japanese War (1905) of the way the Kalmyk Cossacks would overwhelm the Japanese cavalry units by effectively using the *malya* instead of sabers. Clearly, the game described here is more indicative of a spring-time celebration than of marking a new year.

It is interesting to note that the website of the Kalmyk Buddhists (http://khurul.ru/) lists Tsagan Sar as a Kalmyk holiday and not as a Buddhist one, although a shift may be occurring in that interpretation. In his recent collection of Kalmyk legends, D.E. Basaev recounts the following tradition the origin of the Tsagan Sar holiday:

In Honor of the Buddha's Victory!

On the first day of the first spring month Burkhan Bakshi (Shakyamuni Buddha) entered into a debate with six heterodox teachers. This debate lasted for fifteen days. Burkhan Bakshi defeated the heterodox and they accepted his teaching. In honor of this victory a determination was made to commemorate the Tsagan Sar holiday.[9]

Currently, Tsagan Sar is predominantly viewed in Kalmykia as the holiday of the onset of spring. The Kalmyk Buddhist establishment supports that view and the traditions associated with it, but given the existence of a legend that reinterprets the holiday and given the ever-greater urbanization of Kalmyks, perhaps we are seeing the beginning of a different interpretation of the holiday. It will be interesting to see what will eventuate in a generation or two. A partial reinterpretation has already occurred in Mongolia, and the connection to spring appears to have been largely lost among the American Kalmyks.

---

[9] D.E. Basaev. Sem zvezd: kalmytskie legendy i predaniya (*Seven Stars: Kalmyk Legends and Traditions*), Elista: Kalm., Kalm. kn. izd-vo, 2004, st. 76.

DEITIES

Okon Tengri (Heavenly Maiden)

Okon Tengri (pronounced in Kalmyk without the final "i") is a prime deity in Kalmyk and all Mongolian cultures. She is the sky goddess, giver of fire and light, and mother of all. Interestingly, she is considered to be a maiden, somewhat reminiscent of the Virgin Mary in Christianity.

In traditional Kalmyk society fire was the life-giving element and many rituals were practiced to ensure that fire in a home would not be carried out by strangers. Fire was always kept burning in a ger (yurt) because of the belief that extinguishing fire meant ensuing back luck and end of life.

Before Buddhism became the dominant religion of Mongols they had two major deities: Okon Tengri, the "Sky Goddess," and Tsagan Avva (White Elder), the master of the earth. It is interesting that among Mongols the earth deity is male and the sky deity is female, in contrast to some other early religious systems.

In my fieldwork among Kalmyks in Howell, New Jersey, and Philadelphia there was little knowledge about Okon Tengri among the younger generation and virtually no knowledge about Tsagan Avva. Local congregants had a difficult time helping me find icons of Tsagan Avva in the different temples (all of which have one). The Tibetan monks also had very limited knowledge of this deity, since there appears to be no Buddhist or Tibetan counterpart.

Nogan Dara-eke-gegyan (Green Tara)

In Tibeto-Mongolian Buddhism, Tara is a particular female manifestation of an aspect of a Buddha or a bodhisattva. There are several different Taras, each of whom represents a particular quality. Green Tara, one of the most popular of the Taras, is known as the "mother of enlightenment." The deity of enlightened activity, represents success in work and, in Kalmykia, is also viewed as protectress deity. Often her statues or icons represent her with her right hand in an earth-pointing mudra (ritual gesture) and her left hand holding a lotus blossom

All Taras are the female manifestations of Bodhisattva Avolakiteshvara (Chinrezig, Tib.), the bodhisattva of compassion. As such, Taras often share characteristics with the goddess of compassion Kuan Yin, popular in the East Asian traditions.

The veneration of Taras is found in Tibet, Nepal, and among Mongolian people.

Green Tara (Nogan Dara-eke-gegyan) *thangka* at the
Tibetan Buddhist Learning Center, Washington, New Jersey

THE FOLKTALE - TSAGAN SAR[10]

Traditional oral folktales fall into a number of categories that include legends and "fairy" or magic tales. Legends are tales that either recount historical events or involve questions of belief. Magic tales are a subtype of oral folktale, categorized in the famed Aarne-Thompson Tale Type Index under numbers 300 to 749.

A number of legends recount the story of Tsagan Sar, Okon Tengri, and Green Tara. A recent book printed in Kalmykia, *Seven Stars: Kalmyk Legends and Traditions* (2004)[11], presents a few of them. But I have not seen either a magic tale describing the origin of the Tsagan Sar holiday, or one that has two deities as protagonists. There is, of course, a specific category of tales of origins of things, and one for religious tales, but this particular tale seems to be most appropriately classified as "Monster's Bride," and falls squarely into the magic tale category.

The plot of this tale combines a version of the legend of Okon Tengri killing the son of *mangas*—the ogre (devil) and another tale of killing the ogre husband related to the giant's heart in an egg in a Norwegian tale.. In the motif of an external soul, this tale is reminiscent of the famed Russian tales of *Koschei* the Deathless.

The layering of various motifs lies outside the scope of this piece, but it is important to point out that by combining two distinct plots—killing of ogre husband and killing of the son of *mangas*, an interesting change to the legend of Okon Tengri occurs. Instead of the shocking plot element of the deity killing her own son, whom she had with the *mangas*, drinking the dead son's blood, and using his flayed skin as a saddle blanket, in this tale she kills the son of Green Tara with the latter's help. This shift in the plot may represent a shift of people's view of the goddess, or an inability to reconcile the killing of a son with a more modern and less mythic understanding of the tale.

Folktales, particularly magic tales have, over the years, been of interest to scholars of many differing disciplines, ranging from literature to psychoanalysis. Bruno Bettelheim's *The Uses of Enchantment: The Meaning and Importance of Fairy Tales* (1976), which argued for the significance of magic tales in the life and development of children and won critical and popular acclaim, is one of the better known interpretations.

The rise of gender studies has produced many interesting books and studies on the subject of women and magic tales. In her paper, given in the spring of 2012, "Magically Strong Women in Central Asian Wonder Tales and Heroic Tales," Veronica

---

[10] The tale is found in T.G. Basangova. Comp., intro., trans., ref. Sandalovyi larec. Kalmytskie narodye skazki. (*The Sandalwood Treasure Box: Kalmyk Folktales*). Elista: Kalmytskoe knizhnoe izdat-vo. 2002. T.G. Basangova, who is the foremost Kalmyk expert on Kalmyk folktales assigns this tale to the etiological legend genre; I see it differently.

[11] D.E. Basaev. Sem zvezd: kalmytskie legendy i predaniya (*Seven Stars: Kalmyk Legends and Traditions*), Elista: Kalm., Kalm. kn. izd-vo, 2004.

Muskheli brings together around the "Brunhilde" tale type a number of different tales from varied Central Asian countries.

Examining the tale of Tsagan Sar from both psychological and feminist perspectives yields additional understandings. Kalmyk society was organized along patrilineal principles; marriages were exogamic, with the bride leaving for the groom's *khoton*, a nomadic settlement of some 10-12 families. A number of rituals were associated with this departure to ensure that the departing bride would not carry away the family's good luck, contained in the *ger's* fire.

It is, therefore, not accidental that the co-heroine of this tale, Green Tara, is the Bodhisattva of enlightened activity, whose beauty is so intense that one could "graze cattle in her radiance." Her magic "helper" is Okon Tengri, the goddess of fire. Both heroines leave their "people" for the world of the demon *mangas*—the world of strangers and darkness. In addition, the traditional consort of Okon Tengri is Erlik Khan, the ruler of the underworld, who is said to have a powerful body and the face of a pig.

In short, the story tells of a woman who, for the sake of her "people," goes into the world of the dead, destroys death itself (the *mangas* with an external soul), destroys the product of their union to avert a future calamity, and returns, together with the goddess of fire (life), to turn inauspicious days into auspicious ones and bring life and peace to the people. This heroic deed is accomplished at the cost of having to undergo a union with a pig-faced demon, and through the violation of the deepest maternal injunctions by killing, or causing, the death of her own child. This is the tale of a female Prometheus, the creator of mankind, who gave it fire and is eternally punished for having done so. Okon Tengri, in return for sacrificing herself and going into the land of the dead, will eternally ride her mule[12] on a saddle blanket made of her son's flayed skin.

On an everyday, subconscious, psychological level the tale works to help women define positively their apparent secondary status in a deeply patriarchal society by illustrating that marriage to a pig-faced lout could serve their people positively. One thinks that this tale might find particular popularity among women in post-WWII years in the diaspora, where a severe shortage of marriage partners often consigned women to life as a single person or marriage to anything in trousers. Between 1943 and 1957, the choices were few and often grim for Kalmyk women exiled among strangers. It is they, however, who largely kept the home altar lights burning, taught their children what they could, and returned at the first opportunity to their ancestral lands, to rebuild their country and society. This tale contains that story.

---

[12] It is significant that in "canonical" variants of the legend Okon Tengri rides a mule. In the tale we present, however, Nogan Dara-eke-gegyan (Green Tara) and Okon Tengri ride horses; the reasons for that need to be studied further.

CONTRIBUTORS

Eduardo Barrios

Artist. Eduardo Barrios understands journeys and new cultures. In 1969 Eduardo immigrated with his mother and father from Uruguay, South America, to the United States. They spoke only Spanish, feeling like strange people in a strange land. And yet they were cared for, and ministered to, by many kind and generous souls—a generosity he has never forgotten and which informs his way of life and the subject matter of his art.

Eduardo's artistic themes often focus on human affection, mutuality, compassion, connection, and grace. His artistic style is uncomplicated and approachable. A professional graphic designer, he lives in Connecticut with his wife and three children.

In his root faith, Christianity, he offers spiritual guidance to those who seek spiritual perspective and support.

Nikolai Burlakoff

Compiler, translator, and writer. Trained in political science, history, literary studies, folklore, Russian language, and Buddhism, Nikolai has used those skills and that knowledge to convey here a concise vision of Kalmyk spiritual life.

His foray into the world of print began with the publication of a translation of a Russian folktale, "Peter the Great and the Stonemason" and, most recently, a tongue-in-cheek *Kunstmärchen*, or authorial tale, written in imitation of traditional folktales: *Erol Beet and the Borsch Angel.*

His fieldwork observations and research about Kalmyks are presented in Steppe Notes, numbers 1-19, available @ http://www.njfolkfest.rutgers.edu/2011_steppe1.html

Forthcoming are *The World of Borsch/ Мир Борща*, *Kalmyks in America*, and *Buddhism in Russia*, all by AElitaPress.org.

Carleton Copeland

Translator. A native of Detroit, Carleton Copeland fell in love with the Russian language at the University of Michigan. Pursuing his passion to Leningrad in the 1980s, he spent several delirious winters living in ramshackle dormitories, muttering verb conjugations, and wandering the streets of the crumbling imperial capital. The charm has never worn off. He now works as a translator for Ernst & Young in Moscow and spends many evenings and weekends obsessively translating Russian poetry.

Erdni Antonovich Eldyshev

Poet and translator. Graduate of the Kalmyk State University. Member of the Russian Union of Writers. Chair of the governing body of the Kalmyk Union of Writers. Laureate of Literary Awards.

The author of books of poetry: *Native Hearth*, *Morning Flight*, *Seven Cranes*, *Grandpa's Pipe*, and others.

Rimma Khaninova

Poet, playwright, and translator. Graduate of the Kalmyk State University. Holder of a PhD in Philological Studies. Head of the Department of Russian and Foreign Literatures. Writes in Russian. Member of the Russian Union of Writers.

Author of poetry and narrative poem collections: *Winter Rain* (1993), *Soaring Over Worldly Bustle* (1994), *Smart Mouse* (2002), *The Letter "A"* (2010). She also co-authored, with Mikhail Khaninov, *The Hour of Speech* (2002), *I'll Become a Red Tulip* (2010) and, with Ilya Nichiporov, *At the Crossroads of Sophia and Faith* (2005).

She is the author of four monographs about Russian and Kalmyk literature.

The daughter of the well-known Kalmyk poet Mikhail Khaninov (1919-1981), she is the publisher of his literary legacy.

Her personal web site is: www. ханинова.рф

Nicholas Olefer, Jr.

Photographer. The *nom de plume* for photographic works by Nikolai Burlakoff was adopted to honor the life of his stepfather, Nicholas Andreevich Olefer, a first-rate photographer. Nick Olefer Senior's notable photographs include images of a young Bobby Fisher and the aging Judy Garland. A native of Dnipropetrovs'k, Ukraine, Nick Senior was a post-WWII refugee from the USSR, who came to America and built a life based on love, inclusiveness, hard work, and a fierce insistence on individual freedom and clear thinking. He was the proud father of Adrian and Alexander Olefer and happy grandfather of Piper Olefer.

Vera Kirguevna Shugraeva

Poet, playwright, and translator. Graduate of the Stavropol Pedagogical Institute. Member of the Union of Writers of Russia. Laureate of Literary Awards.

She has published over 30 books, including *The Road of Time*, *The Home in Which I Live*, and *Streets of My City*.

14314837R20027

Made in the USA
Charleston, SC
04 September 2012